THE BEST DOGS EVER

YORKSHIRE TERRIERS ARE THE BEST!

Elaine Landau

LERNER PUBLICATIONS COMPANY · MINNEAPOLIS

To Sara Kelly Johns

Lerner Publications Company
A division of Lerner Publishing Group, Inc.
241 First Avenue North
Minneapolis, MN 55401 U.S.A.

Website address: www.lernerbooks.com

Library of Congress Cataloging-in-Publication Data

Landau, Elaine.
    Yorkshire Terriers Are The Best! / by Elaine Landau.
        p.   cm. – (The best dogs ever)
    Includes index.
    ISBN 978-1-58013-557-3 (lib. bdg. : alk. paper)
    1. Yorkshire terrier—Juvenile literature. I. Title.
    SF429.Y6L365 2010
    636.76–dc22   2008021294

Manufactured in the United States of America
1 2 3 4 5 6 – DP – 15 14 13 12 11 10

TABLE OF CONTENTS

CHAPTER ONE

A VERY SPECIAL DOG

Picture a brave, bold dog. Maybe you thought of a huge pooch. Yet the dog I'm thinking of can fit in a shopping bag. It's small but feisty. It's also as cute as a button. People always want to cuddle this dog. It's the pooch they love to smooch.

It's a **Yorkshire terrier,** or **Yorkie.**

What's a Yorkie Like?

Yorkies are much more than just lap dogs. They are active, curious canines. These small dogs are smart and alert. It's hard to get anything past a Yorkie.

Yorkies also have lots of spunk and spirit. At times, they even seem fearless. They often take on much bigger dogs. These pint-sized pooches think big. They don't let their size get in the way.

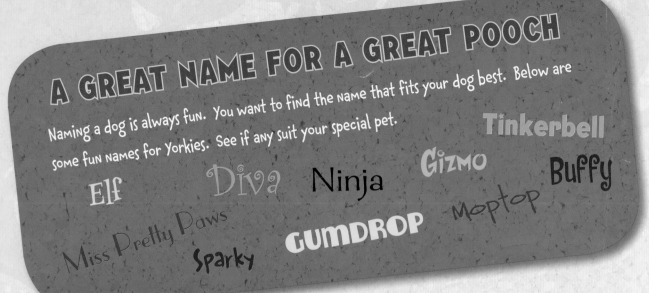

A GREAT NAME FOR A GREAT POOCH

Naming a dog is always fun. You want to find the name that fits your dog best. Below are some fun names for Yorkies. See if any suit your special pet.

Tinkerbell

Elf   Diva   Ninja   Gizmo   Buffy

Miss Pretty Paws   GUMDROP   Moptop

Sparky

Still, Yorkies are among the smallest dogs in the world. They weigh between 4 and 7 pounds (1.8 and 3 kilograms). That's less than a house cat.

Yorkies are also only 7 to 9 inches (17 to 22 centimeters) tall. You probably have stuffed animals bigger than a Yorkie.

Wow! What a Coat!

A Yorkie's coat is long, straight, and silky. It looks and feels like human hair. The Yorkie's coloring is unusual as well. The dog's head and legs are tan. Its body and tail are steel blue.

DOING THE HAIRDO

Did you know that there are special Yorkie hairdos? Many Yorkies have topknots. A topknot is a little like a ponytail. It is tied with a bow in the center of the dog's head.

A Yorkie's hair may also be parted in the middle. Then it's tied on the sides with two bows. Yorkies usually wear red bows.

Yorkies may look like wind-up toys, but they are real dogs. They like doing all the things other dogs do.

Yorkies love being around their owners. They have lots of energy and enjoy play. Yorkies have both charm and character. Their owners think they are the best dogs ever. It's easy to see why.

CHAPTER TWO
YORKIES THROUGH THE YEARS

Have you ever seen photos of Yorkies? These dogs are often posed on silk pillows. Yet Yorkies were not always pampered pooches. They started out as working dogs.

From Scotland to England

In the late 1700s, factories began springing up in England. Workers from nearby countries came to work there. Weavers from Scotland were among them. The Scots brought their small long-haired terriers with them.

These little dogs worked too. They kept mice and rats out of the factories and workers' homes.

SMALL BUT HARDWORKING

Some Yorkies still work in modern times. They are trained therapy dogs. These Yorkies visit hospitals and nursing homes. The patients pet and play with these pooches. The small dogs brighten their day. The Yorkies enjoy their work as well.

Scottish terriers (right) served as rat-catching dogs in England's factories.

A Yorkie makes a beloved pet for this child in the early 1900s.

Over time, the Scottish terriers mixed with other terriers. These dogs were from Yorkshire, England. The end result was the Yorkshire terrier.

By the late 1800s in England, Yorkies had become common household pets. These dogs also did well in dog shows. Many people thought they were sweet. Yet the dogs still had that saucy terrier spirit.

Coming to America

By about 1870, Yorkies were brought to the United States. At first, they were fairly rare in North America. However, in the 1950s, these dogs began to become more common.

In time, more Americans picked Yorkies as pets. Many people just couldn't resist these high-spirited little dogs. These days, Yorkies are among the most popular dogs in the United States.

A New York City woman shops with her Yorkie in 1962.

YORKIES OF THE RICH AND FAMOUS

Some famous people have had Yorkies. Below are just a few of them.

President Richard Nixon had a Yorkie named Pasha.

Actress Audrey Hepburn had a Yorkie named Mr. Famous.

Actress Vanessa Williams (left) has a Yorkie named Enzo.

Toy Dogs

The American Kennel Club (AKC) groups dogs by breed. Some of the AKC's groups include the sporting group, the working group, and the hound group. Yorkies are in the toy group.

This Afghan hound is in the hound group.

Springer spaniels, like this one, are in the sporting group.

This boxer belongs to the working group.

A REAL WINNER

On Valentine's Day in 1978, a Yorkie named Cede Higgins won Best in Show at the Westminster Kennel Club Dog Show. The dog's handler wore a red dress that matched Cede Higgins's red bow. The pair looked perfect for Valentine's Day. This was the first and only time a Yorkie ever won top honors at Westminster.

Dogs in the toy group do not look alike. Yet they have one thing in common. All these dogs are small enough to fit on your lap.

Some people think toy dogs are as cute as can be. Other toy dogs include the pug, the shih tzu, and the Pekingese.

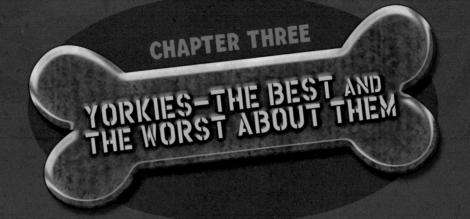

CHAPTER THREE

YORKIES—THE BEST AND THE WORST ABOUT THEM

Just watch a Yorkie strut proudly down the street. Its bright eyes and shiny coat gleam. You could easily become a Yorkie fan. Many people admire these dogs. Yet is a Yorkie really right for you? Read on to find out.

A Small Dog in a Small Space

Do you live in an apartment or condo? Then you might not want a big Great Dane. Instead, a Yorkie might be perfect. These small dogs don't need a lot of space. They take up very little room.

YORKIES AREN'T LONERS

Yorkies don't like to be left alone for long. Do you have many after-school activities? Do the adults in your life work outside the home? If so, a Yorkie may not be for you.

Beware of a Yorkie left alone all day. Lonely Yorkies often get into trouble. These dogs may bark or chew up household items.

A Teeny Tiny Watchdog

Yorkies make great watchdogs. These bold little dogs are fearless. They want to protect their owners. A Yorkie will bark when someone approaches. The dog will also bark if it senses danger.

Some people like having a pint-sized pooch as an alarm system. Others do not. They don't want a dog that barks a lot. How do you feel about it? Does your family feel the same way?

A Yorkie's bark is bigger than its bite!

A Little Exercise for a Little Dog

Large dogs often need lots of exercise. You might spend hours hiking or jogging with a Labrador retriever. It's different with a small dog in the toy group.

A well-paced walk will do fine for a tiny Yorkie. Chasing after the toys you toss to it will also do the trick. So if you're not into hours of exercise, a Yorkie might be right for you.

Handle with Care

Yorkies are sturdy little dogs. However, they are still very small. That means you must be very careful with them.

These dogs can get badly hurt from a fall. They can also be harmed from rough play. If you can't be very gentle with your dog, don't get a Yorkie.

Heavy-Duty Grooming

Are you dazzled by the Yorkie's long, shiny coat? It will take work to get your dog to look that way. Yorkies need a lot of grooming.

You will have to brush and comb your Yorkie's coat daily. You'll also need to bring your Yorkie to the groomer. This can be costly. Be sure your family can afford it.

Some Yorkie owners have their dog's coat trimmed short. This makes grooming easier. Yet these dogs still need to be brushed every day.

Now you know more about Yorkies. Perhaps a Yorkie is the perfect pooch for you. If so, you are lucky. These little dogs make great friends. Yorkies sense their owners' moods. Your Yorkie will always be there for you.

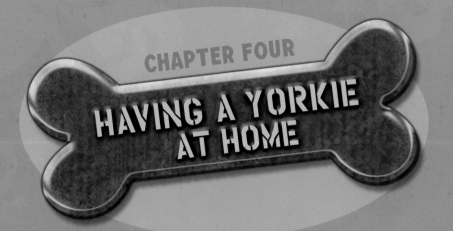

CHAPTER FOUR

HAVING A YORKIE AT HOME

Today's the day you've waited for. You are picking up your Yorkie. It's going to be a day you'll never forget.

Make sure things go smoothly. Be prepared to welcome your new dog home. Have the basic items you'll need. Here is a list of things to get you started:

- collar

- leash

- tags (for identification)

- dog food

- food and water bowls

- crates (one for when your pet travels by car and one for it to rest in at home)

- treats (to be used in training)

- toys

TREATING YOUR YORKIE TO TREATS

Use treats in training your Yorkie. Treats are rewards. Give them to your dog when it does what you ask. Don't offer your Yorkie treats for no reason. Let your pet earn them.

Get to the Vet

A veterinarian, or vet, is a doctor who treats animals. Take your new dog to a vet right away. Your vet will check your pet's health.

At the vet, your dog will also get the shots it needs. You'll see your vet again. Your dog will need more shots later on. And you should take your dog to the vet if it gets sick.

YORKIE HEALTH TIP

Always see that your dog has a bowl of cool, clean water. Don't try to limit the amount of water your dog drinks. This is important for your Yorkie's health.

Feeding Your Yorkie

Give your Yorkie a good-quality dog food. Your dog will need different food at different stages of its life. Ask your vet which is the best food for your Yorkie.

Keep your Yorkie on a dog food diet. Don't give your dog table scraps. This can lead to weight gain and health problems.

How much food is too much? Your vet can tell you how much dog food your Yorkie should have in a day.

You and Your Yorkie

Make time for your Yorkie. Play with your dog every day. Throw a small ball or squeaky toy to your Yorkie. Your dog will joyfully bring it back to you. Yorkies love this game.

FUN AND GAMES WITH YOUR YORKIE

Yorkies like games. Hide a favorite toy under a small towel. Let your dog see you do this. Then say, "Where's the toy?" When your dog goes for it, let your Yorkie have the toy.

In time, make the toy harder to find. Put it under the bed. Try hiding it behind a chair. Yorkies are clever dogs. They enjoy finding the hidden toys.

Your Yorkie will want to go places with you as well. Luckily, Yorkies are tiny. That makes them easy to tote about. Well-trained Yorkies have turned up everywhere. They've been to Little League ball games. These dogs also enjoy going on family picnics.

When you take your dog on an outing, bring water and a dish so your pooch can have a drink.

Many carriers for Yorkies look like handbags, but they are actually made for doggie comfort.

Some Yorkie owners like to dress their dogs in cute outfits. Then they bring their dogs to birthday or holiday parties. Often the Yorkie turns out to be the star guest!

Yorkies are terrific dogs. They make wonderful pets. In return, you owe your Yorkie a great home. Be the best dog owner you can be. The care you give your dog will be well worth it. Yorkies are loving and loyal. Your dog will bring you years of joy.

GLOSSARY

American Kennel Club (AKC): an organization that groups dogs by breed. The AKC also defines the characteristics of different breeds.

breed: a particular type of dog. Dogs of the same breed have the same body shape and general features.

canine: a dog, or having to do with dogs

coat: a dog's fur

diet: the food your dog eats

feisty: very lively, or frisky

groomer: a person who cleans, brushes, and trims a dog's coat

shed: to lose fur

terrier: any of several small, lively dogs

therapy dog: a dog brought to nursing homes and hospitals to comfort patients

toy group: a group of different types of dogs that are all small in size

veterinarian: a doctor who treats animals. Veterinarians are called vets for short.

FOR MORE INFORMATION

Books

Brecke, Nicole, and Patricia M. Stockland. *Dogs You Can Draw*. Minneapolis: Millbrook Press, 2010. This colorful book teaches readers how to draw different kinds of dogs, including the Yorkshire terrier, and shares fun facts about each breed.

Gray, Susan Heinrichs. *Yorkshire Terriers*. Chanhassen, MN: Child's World, 2007. Learn more about Yorkshire terriers in this fun selection.

Landau, Elaine. *Your Pet Dog*. Rev ed. New York: Children's Press, 2007. This title is a good guide for young people on choosing and caring for a dog.

Simon, Seymour. *Dogs*. New York: HarperCollins, 2004. This text offers an interesting look at the intelligence and other characteristics of dogs. Different types of dogs, including terriers and toys, are described.

Stone, Lynn M. *Yorkshire Terriers*. Vero Beach, FL: Rourke Publishing, 2005. Read all about the Yorkie's characteristics and history in this book.

Websites

American Kennel Club
http://www.akc.org
Visit this website to find a complete listing of AKC-registered dog breeds, including Yorkshire terriers. The site also features fun printable activities for kids.

ASPCA Animaland
http://www.aspca.org/site/PageServer?pagename=kids_pc_home
Check out this page for helpful hints on caring for a dog and other pets.

Index

Photo Acknowledgments

The images in this book are used with the permission of: backgrounds © iStockphoto.com/Julie Fisher and © iStockphoto.com/Tomasz Adamczyk; © iStockphoto.com/Michael Balderas, pp. 1, 23 (bottom); © Juniors Bildarchiv/Alamy, pp. 4, 6, 22; © Jose Luis Pelaez Inc/Blend Images/Getty Images, pp. 4-5, 24; © PhotoStockFile/Alamy, p. 5; © Jszg005/Dreamstime.com, pp. 7 (top), 28 (bottom left); © iStockphoto.com/Mikhail Basov, p. 7 (bottom); © Christopher Bissell/Taxi/Getty Images, p. 8; © iStockphoto.com/Steve Shepard, pp. 9, 15; © iStockphoto.com/Eric Isselée, pp. 10, 13 (top right); © Hulton Archive/Getty Images, pp. 10-11; © Mary Evans Picture Library/The Image Works, p. 11; © Yale Joel/Time & Life Pictures/Getty Images, p. 12 (top); © Astrid Stawiarz/Getty Images, p. 12 (bottom); © GK Hart/Vikki Hart/Photodisc/Getty Images, p. 13 (left); © Jerry Shulman/ SuperStock, p. 13 (bottom right); © Mel Yates/Taxi/Getty Images, p. 14; © iStockphoto.com/Teresa Guerrero, p. 16 (top); © Clarissa Leahy/Taxi/Getty Images, p. 16 (bottom); © Image Register 044/ Alamy, p. 17; © Joe McBride/Stone+/Getty Images, pp. 18, 29; © iStockphoto.com/Jodi Jacobson, p. 19; AP Photo/Mary Altaffer, p. 20; © DreamPictures/Riser/Getty Images, p. 21; © Tammy Mcallister/Dreamstime.com, p. 23 (top); © April Turner/Dreamstime.com, p. 23 (second from top); © iStockphoto.com/orix3, p. 23 (second from bottom); © GK Hart/Vikki Hart/The Image Bank/Getty Images, p. 25; © iStockphoto.com/Eric Skorupa, p. 26; © Larry Reynolds/dogpix.com, p. 27 (top); © iStockphoto.com/Joy Fera, p. 27 (bottom); AP Photo/The Saginaw News, Jeff Schrier, p. 28 (top left); © Crystal Kirk/Dreamstime.com, p. 28 (right).

Front Cover: © luchschen-Fotolia.com.
Back Cover: © GK Hart/Vikki Hart/Photodisc/Getty Images.